A NEW ERA
of
PROPHECY
PREPARE TO LISTEN!

A NEW ERA
of
PROPHECY

PREPARE TO LISTEN!

DEVELOP YOUR SPIRITUAL EARS

"Your sons and your daughters shall prophesy"
Joel 2:28; Acts 2:17

"Therefore, consider carefully how you listen"
Luke 8:18, NIV

KAREN BLANKS ADAMS

XULON PRESS

Xulon Press
2301 Lucien Way #415
Maitland, FL 32751
407.339.4217
www.xulonpress.com

© 2021 by KAREN BLANKS ADAMS

All rights reserved solely by the author. The author guarantees all contents are original and do not infringe upon the legal rights of any other person or work. No part of this book may be reproduced in any form without the permission of the author. The views expressed in this book are not necessarily those of the publisher.

Unless otherwise indicated, Scripture quotations taken from the Holy Bible, New International Version (NIV). Copyright © 1973, 1978, 1984, 2011 by Biblica, Inc.™. Used by permission. All rights reserved.

Scripture quotations taken from the King James Version (KJV) – public domain.

Scripture quotations taken from the New King James Version (NKJV). Copyright © 1982 by Thomas Nelson, Inc. Used by permission. All rights reserved.

Scripture quotations taken from the Amplified Bible (AMP). Copyright © 1954, 1958, 1962, 1964, 1965, 1987 by The Lockman Foundation. Used by permission. All rights reserved.

Scripture quotations taken from the New American Standard Bible (NASB). Copyright © 1960, 1962, 1963, 1968, 1971, 1972, 1973, 1975, 1977, 1995 by The Lockman Foundation. Used by permission. All rights reserved.

Scripture taken from The Passion Translation (TPT). Copyright © 2017 by Passion & Fire Ministries, Inc. Used by permission. All rights reserved. thePassionTranslation.com

Printed in the United States of America.

Paperback ISBN-13: 978-1-66280-547-9
eBook ISBN-13: 978-1-6628-0548-6

Table of Contents

Introduction vii

Section 1- Wisdom Comes from God.................. 1
Prepare Your Ear to Hear 11
Active Listening 15
Mastering Active Listening Skills..................... 17

Section 2- How to Hear God's Voice.................. 21
Keys to Study the Bible............................ 25
Develop Your Spiritual Ears 39

Section 3- Learn to Discern the Voice of God........... 41
Why Can't I Hear You, God? 47
God is Speaking: Dreams, Visions, Revelations 48

Section 4- Heart of Worship Opens Windows of Heaven .. 59
Spiritual Hearing to Intercede........................ 67
Strategic Prophetic Intercession 70
Rivers of Living Waters............................ 73
Salvation Prayer................................... 83

**Section 5- God Speaks – Interpreting the World
               Around Us** 85
Root Cause Analysis 88
Methods to Break Strongholds 100
Mind Control Tactics 102

Conclusion 107
References...................................... 111

Introduction

WE HAVE ENTERED ONE OF THE MOST revelatory seasons ever! In October 2019, at the beginning of the Hebrew year 5780, a new ten-year era in which words will have extraordinary prophetic power began. Now, more than ever, we must learn to hear and recognize the voice of God.

We are in a season to speak and declare what God is saying. Our words have power. When God decrees something, it will happen. So too, when people issue a decree, declaration, or proclamation on God's behalf, it will be established (Job 22:28). The media influences millions of people through the power of words to sway public opinions and individual buying habits, beliefs, and views of themselves and others.

A New Era of Prophecy Prepare to Listen!

Every day we see ads on cars, buses, trains, or billboards, and video clips on televisions, computers, and cellphones that we cannot control seeing. Even when we have our phones, computers, or televisions on mute, our minds "hear" what we see. At times, we will have a quick conversation in our heads about what we saw. Advertisers use direct response advertising to lure us into making impulsive purchases based upon what we see.

Response advertising is a marketing tool designed to compel us to have an internal conversation about the ads we see. It usually is a quick conversation, such as, "That is good to know. I will have to google that when I have time." Sometimes, we have an extended discussion in our heads, "discussing" what we saw, such as, "I have to have that!" "Yeah, but where is the money coming from to get it?" "I will charge it." "But you don't need it." And so, it goes. We all "hear" with our eyes.

Most people agree, as humans, we have a mind, body, and spirit. We have physical ears; we also have spiritual ears. We all have intelligence (brainpower) and

Introduction

discernment (spiritual insight). We all listen to voices. We all respond, on some level, to what we hear.

The question is, "Whose voice are you listening to?"

In my book *Life in the Matrix: Are you really in control of your decisions?* I wrote a chapter titled "Universal Unconsciousness," in which I wrote about how our belief systems and worldviews at a minimum influence and at an extreme control how we respond to what we hear.

Time after time in the news or on the Internet, we hear or read stories about people "hearing voices" that told them to act in certain ways. The negative implications of "hearing voices" have resulted in many belief systems and worldviews that reject even the possibility that God speaks. The truth is—God is alive. He speaks to us.

Hearing with our spiritual ears gives us the ability to visualize and draw blueprints of God's vision for the plans He gives us. For example, in 1 Chronicles 28:2, 3, 11, 12 (NIV), King David describes how the Spirit put in his mind plans to "build a house as a place of rest

A New Era of Prophecy Prepare to Listen!

for the ark of the covenant of the LORD." Just as God communicated with King David, He will speak to you.

Have you ever had dreams, visions, or intuitions that spoke to your mind, and you did not know what to do or how to do it? Or you *knew* in your heart, you were called to do something but did not know how to proceed? Or felt in your spirit that you were to go and do something but allowed fear, doubt, or anxiety to keep you from going? If so, then this book is a must-read for you.

Proven methods to improve your active listening skills are detailed in this book. Guidelines on how prophetic people meditate on and study the Word of God are shared. You will read examples of how, during our everyday lives, people hear and act in response to hearing the voice of God.

This book will help you to "listen to hear the Voice of God." After reading this book, you will know how to:

1. Call to God so He will answer you;
2. Recognize His voice;

Introduction

3. Develop strategies to act on the revelation you receive from God.

It is my prayer for you to be as eager to hear the voice of God as He is to answer you. Let those who have ears to hear—listen. God loves us, and He wants to communicate with us and through us!

Section One

Wisdom Comes From God

> *But if any of you lacks wisdom, you should pray to God, who will give it to you, because God gives generously and graciously to all.*
> (James 1:5, GNB)

IN THE INTRODUCTION OF THIS BOOK, I wrote, "We have entered one of the most revelatory seasons ever! In October 2019, at the beginning of the Hebrew year, 5780, a new ten-year era in which words will have extraordinary prophetic power began. Now, more than ever, we must learn to hear and recognize the voice of God."

A New Era of Prophecy Prepare to Listen!

During this new and exciting season of speaking, God increases our sensitivity and understanding of how He speaks. God is awakening our ears to hear the numerous ways of hearing Him. God is amplifying our senses to discern the variety of ways He speaks. I recently read a book titled *"God is My Banker: Spiritual Strategies for Entrepreneurs"* by Gwen Osborne. In the introduction, she wrote,

> *As you read this book, you will notice I often "hear" the Lord speak or "see" things He shows me. To some, this may seem strange, even unbelievable…Sometimes, I hear Him in my spirit, sometimes the written Word burns through my veins, sometimes I see pictures so packed with revelation I could write a book. Rarely do I hear an audible voice, but what I do hear is loud and clear. I cannot adequately explain how these things happen, except by the Spirit of the Living God, who dwells in*

> *me. This kind of insight and communication is available to all who desire to know the Lord.... God wants to have a deep relationship with anyone who will participate, and communication is part of any relationship. The point being everyone can have the same experience I do. It just requires a tad of faith and practice hearing.*

Communication is an essential part of any relationship. God wants to have a close relationship with us—He is the only source of true wisdom.

God wants to share His wisdom with us. When we bring our concerns, troubles, and questions to God, expecting His answers and guidance, He will respond. *God is more eager to answer than we are to ask.*

God will heighten our natural ability to hear His response by disclosing His mind, will, and purpose for the specific situation or immediate need. Suddenly, a thought will come to mind that instructs, guides, and brings peace to move forward.

A New Era of Prophecy Prepare to Listen!

I remember a time when God suddenly spoke to me. My husband and I had relocated to another city. We wanted to find a new home church. As we were driving to a church of a nationally well-known minister, in my mind, I "heard" a voice speak loud and clearly say, "Turn here!" I immediately told my husband, "Turn here." We were driving past a church at that moment. He asked, "Why?" I said, "God said, 'Turn here,' so turn here."

My husband turned into the parking lot of the church. He asked me what I knew about the church. I told him I did not know anything about the church. God said, "Turn here," so that is why we will go to this church. He reluctantly agreed to go into the church but believed I had heard from God since we were driving past a church when I heard God say, "Turn here."

We went into the church and sat in the back row. This church was a non-denominational Apostolic/Prophetic church that taught on the spiritual gifts found in 1 Corinthians 12 and the Five-Fold Ministry—apostles, prophets, evangelists, pastors, and teachers found in Ephesians 4:8–13.

The church we were initially driving to was a traditional Bible fellowship church that strongly believed in teaching the Word of God but did not believe there are modern-day apostles and prophets. We had never heard of or knew about apostolic/prophetic churches before attending this church. During the service, the prophet/pastor walked to the back of the church and told us, "The Lord said for you to get rooted and get grounded."

We were amazed. Although we had just relocated to Texas, my husband had received a job offer earlier in the week to move to Kansas. I did not want to move again, but my husband wanted to accept the promotion and move. When we heard the prophetic word to get rooted and get grounded, we both knew God was telling us not to move to Kansas. We knew God wanted us to "get rooted and get grounded" in Texas and become actively involved in church. This prophetic word resonated with us. My husband respectfully declined the job offer. After we attended a few more services, we joined that church.

By listening to the words spoken by God through the pastor, God placed us on a path that changed our lives and heightened our spiritual knowledge and understanding by leaps and bounds. By being obedient and responding in faith when God said, "Turn here" and to "Get rooted and get grounded," we entered a new season of spiritual growth that propelled us into our future.

> *For the revelation awaits an appointed time; it speaks of the end and will not prove false. Though it lingers, wait for it; it will certainly come and will not delay* (Habakkuk 2:3).

Be assured, when we seek God, He will respond. God will speak to us in outward ways, such as messengers (pastors, prophets, teachers, coworkers, neighbors, ministers), angels, or even through a donkey (Numbers 22:28) or a burning bush (Exodus 3:2–6).

God will speak to us through circumstances, divine connections, or divine appointments, such as when God said to me at the appointed time directing me to

"Turn here" into the parking lot of the church I mentioned above.

God, through the Holy Spirit, will speak to us through our prayers and intercession (Romans 8:26, 27). God will supernaturally increase our faith beyond our natural ability to believe for a change in specific matters and areas of concern. God will guide our prayers for people, places, businesses, or any situation or circumstance to bring about change. Slowly or suddenly, a change will occur. What seems impossible or unlikely to change will change. With God, all things are possible!

It is not always easy to have confidence and believe in what seems to be impossible. When doubts overtake you, ask God to increase your faith. Trust God to hear and answer your prayer. It may take time to see the change. Keep praying and believing. God will reveal His mind, will, and purpose for your specific situation or need and give you peace.

BLOCKED EARS

At times, you may not be able to hear God's voice. There is an ear condition referred to as "blocked ears," which temporarily causes a loss of hearing. It can occur at high altitudes or while scuba diving. A person's hearing becomes muffled, causing the person not to hear clearly.

Hearing from God can, at times, be compared to blocked ears. His voice may become muffled by daily distractions, concerns, family, friends, work, ministries, volunteering assignments, or other worries or cares of the world, which clog our minds and keep us from hearing clearly. During those times, take a break to praise, worship, pray, or read scriptures to unblock your spiritual ears to listen to His voice.

Allow the peace of God to fill you with the knowledge of His will in all wisdom and spiritual understanding. By spending intimate time with God, you will unclog your ears and hear and recognize God's voice.

God will open your ears and heart to receive specific strategies to achieve a breakthrough.

ATTENTION DEFICIT DISORDERS

In the natural, there is a condition that impairs a person's listening skills called attention deficit hyperactivity disorder (ADHD). Physical characteristics of ADHD are difficulty paying attention, excessive, inappropriate activity, and acting without regard to consequences.

I believe there is a similar condition in the spirit realm. I call it spiritual attention deficit hyperactivity disorder. Spiritual ADHD impairs a person's mind from hearing the voice of God. The person has difficulty paying attention when others are speaking the truths contained in the Bible. The person becomes fidgety and, at times, walks out of sermons or walks away from conversations about God. They may act in sinful, destructive, or inappropriate ways without regard to the consequences.

Manifestations of spiritual ADHD are evident throughout our society today. Social media has created a "selfie" mentality that diverts a person's attention from God to self. Although God is speaking through words, songs, and creation itself, social media can control what people hear and influence how they think. Over time, oppositional behavior toward God grows, causing some people to choose not to hear God's voice. They may impulsively join organizations or groups that actively try to silence the voice of God in all forms of communication.

In this era of speaking, free speech is increasingly becoming restricted. In many cities in America and countries worldwide, laws and regulations ban the truth found in the Bible.

Spiritual ADHD can happen to anyone. Even the most highly regarded apostles, prophets, evangelists, pastors, and teachers (Ephesians 4:11) must focus on hearing the voice of God. They must stop what they are doing, silence distractions, and actively attune their spiritual ears to listen to the voice of God. They, too, can succumb to the views opposed to the truth found in the Bible and embrace ungodly laws and practices.

Spiritual ADHD may temporarily impair a person's mind from being receptive to hearing God's wisdom, knowledge, understanding, and wise counsel. But God!

To God belong wisdom and power; counsel and understanding are His (Job 12:13). God will give us ears to hear. He will remove all obstacles that attempt to block our ears from hearing. *God is eager to share His wisdom with us!*

PREPARE YOUR EAR TO HEAR

Then Jesus said, "Whoever has ears to hear, let them hear" (Mark 4:9).

Choose to believe God will generously and graciously give wisdom and revelation to all who ask for it. Wisdom is what to do. Revelation is how to do it. Ask God for guidance. Then eagerly wait and listen for God to respond.

When God speaks, listen. Ask Him questions to clarify what you do not understand. Have a thoughtful conversation with God. He will respond. He wants you to hear and understand what He is saying.

I like to have tea with Jesus. I prepare a cup of tea, sit at the table with a notepad, and ask Him questions. I listen with my mind and write His responses. I jot down all thoughts that come to mind. When I feel He has told me everything He wants to say to me at that time, I stop writing and meditate on what I have written. Sometimes, I know I have received my marching orders, and I move forward. At other times, I do not fully understand how to proceed.

Hearing does not always mean comprehending. Comprehension is the ability to understand something. People can hear and not understand. Although they are listening, they do not hear or understand (Matthew 13:13). In them is fulfilled the prophecy of Isaiah:

> *You will be ever hearing but never understanding; you will be ever seeing but never*

> *perceiving. For this, people's hearts have become calloused; they hardly hear with their ears, and they have closed their eyes. Otherwise, they might see with their eyes, hear with their ears, understand with their hearts and turn, and I (Lord Jesus) would heal them.* (Matthew 13:14–15)

When I do not understand, I pause and reflect on why I do not understand. I ask myself, Has my heart become hardened? During one of these times of reflection, God took me to Psalm 36. I read the entire chapter and could not see how this Psalm related to me. Then, I read it one sentence at a time and thought about it. The first two sentences are:

> *"I have a message from God in my heart concerning the sinfulness of the wicked: There is no fear of God before their eyes. In their own eyes, they flatter themselves too much to detect or hate their sin"* (Psalm 36:1, 2).

I realized my arrogance kept me from detecting the things I was doing that displeased God. God led me through each verse to reveal my self-righteousness, my hypocrisy, my willful disobedience. I listened and heard the message from God in my heart concerning my wickedness. It was very humbling. I repented and declared Psalm 36:9 over myself, "In Your light, Lord, I see the light."

LISTENING IS ACTIVE

Listening is active. It is not just hearing or perceiving sounds. Listening is tuning out distractions and tuning in to what is essential. Begin each day in prayer to prepare yourself to hear God's voice actively through sights, sounds, tastes, smells, and feelings. Pray to demolish arguments and every pretension that sets itself up against the knowledge of God (2 Corinthians 10:5).

Still your mind and allow God to prepare you for the day ahead. Linger in God's presence for a while before plunging into your daily activities. Play worship music while you get dressed. Listen to the Bible or worship music while you are in the car or on the bus or subway. Prepare your spirit for the day.

As you go through your day, listen for God's voice wherever you go. He will speak to you in various ways. Ideas will suddenly pop into your mind. Thoughts will come to you that will provide solutions to problems or concerns troubling you. God is speaking. Enjoy the intimate counsel of the Lord. (Psalm 25:14, ISV)

ACTIVE LISTENING

Listening can be one of the hardest things to do consistently. It takes practice to become an active listener. In the business world, listening is considered the single most important communication skill. It is valued more highly than speaking.

Speaking is relatively easy to do. At times, we compete for our turn to talk and fail to listen to what others are saying. We are thinking about our response to express our thoughts, feelings, or purposes while the other person is speaking. It takes effort to deliberately clear our minds and concentrate our focus on the speaker.

Active listening requires us to listen with not only our ears but also with our eyes and minds. Verbal, visual, and mental messages are continuously transmitted. When we see, we listen. When we read, we listen. Seeing or reading also does not necessarily include comprehending.

We regularly view and read e-mails, text messages, books, or other forms of written communications provided by others. However, we often do not understand the message others are trying to convey.

We live in a world filled with distractions. Active listening is about tuning out distractions and tuning in to what is vital. Therefore, we must train ourselves to discern nonverbal communication to understand the message beyond the message seen or heard on the surface to grasp what lies beneath.

The seeds sown through communication continue to grow. Night and day, the seeds sprout and grow.

Though you may not know it, the seeds take root in your thoughts producing beliefs that influence your decisions. Ideas are sown, which lead to good choices, bad choices, or tragic results, which is why it is important to process what you hear carefully.

Listen with your ears. Understand with your heart. Discern using God's knowledge.

MASTER THE ART OF LISTENING

Listening to pay attention can be difficult, but you can master it with practice. There are three primary reasons many of us have not yet mastered the art of listening.

1. We do not tune out distractions, such as external (e.g., all the texts and notifications popping up on our phones while we study, meditate, read the Bible, attend meetings) or internal (i.e., all those thoughts in our heads).

2. We do not *wan*t to listen. We do not want to know the truth. By paying closer attention, we might find out we were wrong when we hoped we were right. Consider our relationships with others and how hard it can be to learn we were wrong about someone or something.
3. We focus on getting our voices heard rather than listening. (e.g., we talk over others when they are speaking, we finish someone else's sentence expressing our views rather than letting the other person finish, we interrupt the speaker by asking a "clarifying question," which is a commonly used tactic to state our ideas).

Poor listening skills can, in part, be a result of mimicking how talk show hosts, newscasters, or sports analysts conduct themselves during their broadcasts. They often talk over one another to get their point across. Even when they agree, they still interrupt each other to voice their views. This form of communication subconsciously teaches viewers that speaking is more important than listening. The result is many of us struggle to listen.

When someone is speaking, ask yourself, "Am I paying attention, listening, and comprehending? Or was I thinking about my response?" Be honest with yourself. These questions can help you to improve your listening skills.

Not listening can cause us to miss critical pieces of communication, both positive and negative. It can take us down error-filled paths because we failed to heed warning signs. Not listening can mean the difference between success or failure. By practicing the tips below, we can become good listeners.

- Listen actively and empathetically to the views and concerns of others.
- Welcome the opportunity to hear competing points of view.
- Do not take criticism personally. Listen to hear and understand.

- Repeat what was said to clarify what you believe you heard.
- Take time to interpret and understand the context, motives, and reasoning in received communications.
- Ask questions.
- Remember to pause and let others finish what they have to say before you respond.

Listening is also about knowing when there is no other information beyond what is on the surface and recognizing there is no need to dig deeper for hidden messages.

Spend time during the next week to assess how well you listen. Engage in the above behaviors more frequently than you do now. See what differences result in your communications with others. Listening is difficult. However, you can master active listening with practice.

Section Two

How to Hear God's Voice

GOD SPEAKS TO YOU EVERY DAY. HE longs to have a personal relationship with you. God designed you and me to have relationships, and communication is a big part of a thriving relationship. But how? How does God speak, and how can we know we have heard His voice?

One of the most powerful ways to hear God's voice is through the Bible. Paul wrote to Timothy, "All Scripture is inspired by God and is profitable for teaching, for reproof, for correction, and instruction in righteousness" (2 Timothy 3:16).

When I was in my twenties, I heard a voice in my mind that said, "You read every new bestseller novel that is released, but you have never read the Bible. Before you read another book, I want you to read the Bible." I knew the voice was right.

I had attended church since I was a child. I believed in Jesus and got baptized when I was a child. I had participated in Sunday school and been taught the Ten Commandments and read popular stories from the Bible, such as the birth of Jesus in a manger, Noah and the Ark, and David and Goliath. We celebrated Easter and Christmas. I sang in the choir.

I carried my Bible to church every week. The minister would begin every sermon telling us to "turn your Bible to…" He would read a verse or two from the Bible and proceed to preach for about an hour. His message would be very moving, and at times, entertaining. But we would not look at our Bibles again for the remainder of the service. I realized, although I had been in church since I was a child, I did not know much about what was written in the Bible because I had never read it.

Immediately after God told me to read the Bible, I purchased a King James Version of the Bible and began to read it like a novel. I was determined to read it from the beginning to the end, like reading a book. I found it hard to understand but struggled through it in obedience to what God told me to do.

By God's grace, I mentioned what I was doing to a couple I played doubles tennis with every week. Although we played tennis, we had never talked about God. The following week, the wife brought me a New Testament Bible of the New American Standard Version of the *Ryrie Study Bible*.

This magnificent gift opened my eyes and heart to the word of God. The words were in modern language, not the old-style language found in the King James Version. It was easy to read. The footnotes explained the Bible in a way that made it enjoyable to read. For Christmas that year, I asked my family to give me a *Ryrie Study Bible*, which included both the Old and New Testament. They all chipped in and purchased a leather-bound copy for me. It has always been my favorite Christmas gift. I still own and cherish it.

As I read and meditated on the Bible, certain scriptures would speak directly to my heart. I became a Sunday school teacher for adult classes because I knew many young and old adults did not read or did not understand the word of God. One important lesson I learned through this experience is that not all adults know how to read. I learned to ask, "Who would like to read the next section of the lesson?" rather than calling upon a specific person to read.

As a teacher, it is essential to be sensitive and not inadvertently embarrass members of the class. In today's society, there are many high school dropouts. Some teenagers and adults do not know how to read, or they have limited reading skills. We always want everyone to feel welcomed to learn about the Lord.

Even for those who can read, it is not always easy to understand the Bible. Fortunately, there are several easy to read and understand translations of the Bible. You can quickly download a Bible app that contains various translations on your phone. In addition to a Bible app, you will still want to purchase or download a study

Bible. A study Bible includes notes which provide historical information about the authors of each book of the Bible, geographical locations, customs and traditions, and in-depth commentary concerning the content of each of the books in the Bible.

God speaks to everyone through His words written in the Bible. His Holy Spirit will awaken your spirit to the revelation contained within the Bible. A *Life Application Study Bible* is an excellent Bible that will help you understand how to apply what you read to your daily life. Your life will change by meditating on and studying the Word of God.

KEYS TO STUDY THE BIBLE

Read each passage of scripture. Pause. Meditate on what you read.

1. Ask God, What He sees.
2. Ask God, What He meant.

3. Ask God, What He wants you to understand from each passage.

During your daily Bible study, as you read, look for patterns and write them down. Often you will find that God is speaking in response to something which may be troubling you. For example, during a difficult season when I asked God for guidance, Psalm 27 was placed on my heart, which I meditated on frequently. I found great comfort in Psalm 27.

Often, God responds by leading me to verses in the Bible that say things like, "Teach me to do your will, for you are my God; may your good Spirit lead me on level ground" (Psalm 143:10). Or "I instruct you in the way of wisdom and lead you along straight paths" (Proverbs 4:11). These scriptures reassure me God is leading me and leveling the path before me. I can trust Him to guide me and show me what to do.

Like me, you, too, can and will hear God's voice by reading the Bible. When you are troubled by something, read the Bible. The Lord will speak directly to you from His Word. You will read a Scripture that will jump out at you like a flashing neon light. It will provide an answer to a question or concern you have. It will encourage you and give you hope. It will calm you. It will fill you with peace.

In Psalm 32:8, it says, "I will instruct you and teach you in the way which you should go." God instructs us through the Bible, through supernatural inspiration received from the Holy Spirit, through other people, such as a pastor's sermon, a friend's wise counsel, a parent's words of encouragement or rebuke, or a prophetic word spoken by one of God's Spirit-filled servants.

Memorize key verses in the Bible that speak to you so they will come to mind when you need them. Your memory scriptures will bring you strength, peace, and comfort, in times of need.

THE GIFT OF PROPHECY

Prophecy is speaking the mind and heart of God, as revealed by the Holy Spirit. God often speaks to us through other people. A prophetic word can come in the form of comfort, encouragement, exhortation, or direction.

Prophecy can also be redemptive, communicating God's planned purpose for a person or a territory. God wants us to know His plans and intentions for our lives and the communities where we live.

A message delivered in a sermon, or seminar, or class, or even during a conversation can contain divine knowledge or wisdom that speaks to us. When God speaks to us in this way, in our hearts, we know He is talking.

When God reveals His mind and heart to us, we may have a strong feeling to move ahead concerning plans we have been mulling over. We may feel a burden lift as we receive the answer to a troubling problem or concern. We may feel a sense of peace that calms our spirit.

The Bible has a lot to say about peace. A search of the word "peace" in the Bible reveals numerous ways to receive God's peace. One of my favorite verses is, "In peace, I will lie down and sleep, for you alone, LORD, make me dwell in safety" (Psalm 4:8). Each night before I sleep, I thank God for His protection and trust Him to keep me safe.

Throughout the Bible, God used prophets and others to warn people and deliver messages to encourage, instruct, and correct during good times and times of need. Even today, God continues to speak through people to share His plans. For it is written, "Surely the Sovereign LORD does nothing without revealing his plan to his servants the prophets" (Amos 3:7).

God is always available to us. He knows the plans He has for us, and He wants us to enjoy those plans. God wants us to listen to Him and obey Him. When we submit our concerns to God in prayer, He will answer. (Jeremiah 33:3)

Distractions are a hindrance to receiving revelation. Ask God to tune your ears to His heavenly frequency and to remove all interference so that you can hear His voice. Then listen to Him and follow His guidance and instructions. If God is asking you to change—change. If

God is asking you to start or finish an assignment—do it. If God is asking you to go somewhere—go.

LEARN TO DISCERN THE VOICE OF GOD

Listen and learn to discern the voice of God. Receiving divine guidance is not difficult when you sincerely want to hear God's voice. God still speaks by His Holy Spirit through a message of wisdom, or a word of knowledge, or through prophecy. (1 Corinthians 12:8, 10)

God warns us to be cautious when people tell us, "I have a message from the LORD" because the message may not be from Him (Jeremiah, 23:26). For example, a person may know you want to get married, so the person "prophesies" you will marry someone, possibly a specific person, by stating, "The Lord says."

God gives us the ability to discern if the message is from Him. The message not only will encourage, strengthen, or comfort you, it will resonate with your spirit. If you have a "check" in your mind, pray over the prophetic word. Ask God if it is His message or a message from the speaker's soul. Sometimes, a well-meaning person will attempt to comfort you and may honestly believe the words are a message from God when, in fact, the words did not originate from God.

At times, it may be difficult for us to hear God's voice. The inability to discern God's voice could be due to debates, confusion, conflict, disagreement, or simply not knowing the voice of God. During those times, fasting, praying, and worshipping will bring us into God's presence.

Praise changes the atmosphere. As we praise God, He brings our spirit into perfect union with the Holy Spirit, and it becomes easier to hear His voice. The Holy Spirit will give us divine revelation in response to our prayer requests.

Be careful not to let *joy robbers* stop you from experiencing God's best. If you feel your joy is dwindling, ask God to release an anointing of gladness. Allow God to fill you with His love and joy that overflows, a peace that subdues, patience that endures, kindness in action, a life full of virtues, faith that prevails, the gentleness of heart, and limitless self-control. (Galatians 5:22, 23, TPT)

When you worship, pray, or fast, pause and consider, "What is Holy Spirit speaking to me?" Write it down. Meditate on what you wrote. If you received instructions, follow those instructions. If you are unclear on what to do, ask God for help. For example, suppose God says to you, "Open a healing room." You may have questions about where to open it, how to establish it, or how to let people know it exists. When you listen, obey, and believe, God will provide the help you need to accomplish His plans. After all, it is God's healing room! Holy Spirit will bring to mind people to contact who can guide and assist you.

HOW TO HEAR THE VOICE OF GOD

Following are some ways to prepare and to hear God's voice:

- Be still! Allow the concerns of the day to settle. Calm your mind.
- Remove distractions.
- Look! Put your focus on God. Allow God to open the eyes of your heart.
- Mental visions—pictures may come to mind that speaks to you. This is especially true of artistic, creative people. God speaks through creation.
- Listen for God's voice. Ask questions concerning what is troubling you. How do you perceive His response? Write it down.
- Read the Bible.
- Pray God's Word out of the scriptures you read. Pray the answer.
- Practice hearing God's voice for yourself and others.

When you call out to God, He will answer (Jeremiah 33:3). God wants to communicate with you!

GUIDANCE FROM TRUSTED ADVISERS

Plans fail for lack of counsel, but with many advisers, they succeed. (Proverbs 15:22)

At times God speaks through others, such as our parents, spouses, pastors, bosses, peers, consultants, mentors, or close friends. The wise writer of Proverbs wrote, "Victory is won through many advisers" (Proverbs 11:14). In response to your prayers, God will place people on your path to help you.

I can recall when I needed to change insurance carriers for the liability insurance coverage at the organization where I worked. I was new to the organization. I was in charge of risk management. During our first cycle of policy renewals, I discovered the current insurance broker had not sought competitive bids for our liability insurance for years; therefore, the insurance premiums had increased annually for the past few years. Although our organization had not filed any claims in years, our broker did not question the increases or attempt to lower our costs. Our insurance premiums were extremely high.

The status quo existed due to the relationship the insurance agent had with the organization. I expressed my concerns to my boss. After meeting with our insurance agent and attempting to lower our costs to no avail, my boss and I agreed to search for a new insurance broker to handle our policies. Due to the timing, we had to renew the current insurance policies at the higher rates before the existing policies expired. The organization was a Christian university. We prayed for wisdom and committed our plans to the Lord. (Proverbs 16:3)

Miraculously, our university's president attended a fundraiser during the time of the renewals. During the event, one of the attendees at the fundraiser, a senior vice president in the insurance services division at a large insurance company, approached our president and advised him he would like to speak with us about our insurance. Our president gave his business card to my boss and asked us to contact him. As a result of this divine appointment, we were able to switch brokers, cancel our existing policies, and lower our insurance liability costs by more than forty percent!

When you are wrestling with a big decision, ask God for guidance. If you are having trouble hearing God, ask Him why. It could be He is answering you, and you are not listening. When God's answer is no, and that is not the answer you want to hear, it can be challenging to accept you are hearing from God. One way you will know is you will ask others what they think and receive many confusing answers.

In the Book of Galatians (1:9), we read, "Evidently some people are throwing you into confusion and trying to pervert the gospel of Christ." Just as some people were trying to pervert the gospel of Christ, some people will try to cause you to reject the no you heard from the voice of God and do something that is against what God is saying. It is important to stop and pray and not let confusion guide you into making an unwise decision.

On the other hand, you could know God spoke to you, but you do not know how to do what God wants you to do. For example, God may want you to start a new ministry, but you do not know how to do it. Or God may be telling you to make some lifestyle changes. You may need to call trusted advisors for advice on how to do what God is telling you to do. If it is a personal decision, consult with people who know you best. If it is a business decision, consult with experts in the field. Consult with people who hear from God. Ask intercessors to agree to pray with you to seek God's counsel and allow them to speak into your decision.

Life is complicated. Often there are significant decisions in which you want to be sure you have heard God correctly. Discuss your concerns with others. Seek wise counsel and support from your church community as you do your best to hear God's voice. Discernment on a particular issue will often come to those in your inner circle as each one seeks the Lord's face. When you believe you have gathered as much input as possible, submit your decision to God in prayer. Ask God how does He feel about your decision. Fast, pray, and allow God to guide you. He will clear the road for you to follow! (Proverbs 3:5, 6)

FAITH INVOLVES RISK

When God speaks, we may need to take a risk and grow deeper in our faith. Here's the thing about bold faith: it involves risk. When you are trying to determine if you heard the voice of God correctly, ask yourself, "What is the way of faith?" If it involves faith, you can almost guarantee God is speaking. Faith comes by hearing, and hearing comes by the word of God. (Romans 10:17)

Set aside time daily to spend with God. Spend time listening for His guidance as you read, study, and meditate while reading the Bible. Document the things which speak to your heart. Record biblical promises and hold fast to them, knowing God keeps His promises. Make a note of any conditions within the biblical promises, such as, if you obey God, you will be blessed (see Deuteronomy 28:1–14).

Give thanks to God, who can do exceedingly abundantly beyond all we ask or think, according to the power that works within us (Ephesians 3:20). The Holy Spirit of God is the power that works within us. He abides in everyone who confesses with their mouth and believes in their heart that Jesus Christ is the Son of God, whom God raised from the dead (Romans 10:8–10).

Receive God's gift of salvation. Experience His spiritual gifts. Learn to listen and discern with your spiritual senses. Following are some things to remember when God speaks:

- Journal/review prophetic words; they are a message from the heart of God (Amos 3:7)
- Choose obedience. When God speaks—obey. No matter what—obey (Dt. 5:33; Ps. 128:1)

WAYS TO DEVELOP YOUR SPIRITUAL EARS

1. Examine Yourself (Psalm 36)
   a. Do you detect hate?
   b. Do you detect sin?
   c. Do you fail to act wisely?
   d. Do you choose to act wisely?

e. Do you reject what is wrong?
2. Pause a moment; let the noise go away; listen to God's voice
3. Do not be distracted by outside sounds
4. Be in harmony—tuned in to God's voice
5. Listen to the various expressions of the Holy Spirit (1 Corinthians 12:7, 8)
   a. You will know when one cycle ends, and it is time to shift (Ecclesiastes 3:1)
   b. You will know when it's time to store away for another time, another season, another day (Ecclesiastes 3:6)
6. Hear God's Word and put it into practice. (Luke 8:21)

Section Three

Learn to Discern the Voice of God

MANY VOICES ARE COMPETING FOR YOUR attention. Whose voice are you listening to—parents, spouses, siblings, friends, internet, music, television, billboards, social media? All these voices are competing for your attention to influence your behavior. How do you filter those voices to make wise choices? Through popular worldviews? Or through the Word of God?

In Luke 8:4–15, Lord Jesus teaches a parable about seeds sown by a farmer. Some of the seeds fell along the path and were trampled; some fell on rocky ground and withered away; some fell among thorns and were choked, and some fell on good soil and yielded a crop a hundred times more than was sown. Lord Jesus used this parable to teach about the Word of God.

Lord Jesus called out to the people saying, "Whoever has ears to hear, let them hear." He warned there would be people who "though seeing, they may not see; though hearing, they may not understand" (Luke 8:10). He explained the seed sown is the word of God. The parable's purpose was to describe how the revelation in God's word will affect people differently. It will take root in some people and not others.

The multitude of voices around us can impair, impede, or silence the Word of God. These voices can shape our views and lead us to compromise or reject the truths contained in the Bible. We are in a season in which it is essential to have ears to hear and understand. Careful self-examination will help you to avoid unwise words or actions brought on by listening to internal or external voices that plant negative thoughts and ungodly beliefs.

Examine yourself. Ask the question, "Is there anything in my life that hinders my belief or faith in the Word of God or obedience to God?" If so, humble yourself before God and ask God to help you to overcome life's temptations.

God promises to help us overcome every temptation: "You are tempted in the same way that everyone else is tempted. But God can be trusted not to let you be tempted too much, and He will show you how to escape from your temptations" (1 Corinthians 10:13, CEV).

God is on your side! He will help you to overcome every challenge you face.

A MEASURE OF REVELATION

My husband, Leeman Adams, wrote the following in the thesis he submitted in partial fulfillment of the requirements for the degree of master of theological studies in 2012:

> God does nothing without revealing it first to His servants, the prophets. So it is important to understand how time and space are related to revelation when you

receive revelation. God will only reveal events and knowledge that is associated with the portion that He has given you. Normally, you will not receive revelation that is outside of your boundaries. When God is going to change or expand your portion, He will let you know.

How important is revelation? In the book *Spiritual Authority,* Watchman Nee (Nee, 1972) writes, "The value of a man is not determined by the judgment of others, but by the measure of revelation he received from God. Authority is built upon the revelation one has received from God. Great revelation is evidence of a relationship and brings great spiritual authority. When God stops speaking revelation, our favor and authority is rejected. An open heaven over our lives is a testimony of God's favor and authority resting upon us.

I am so accustomed to God speaking to me (Leeman Adams) that it is very noticeable when He stops. God stopped speaking to me several years ago, and I had to determine why, what did I do wrong, or what had I not done. I reviewed the dreams that God had given me and realized that I was in disobedience. God had told me to leave the church I was attending and join another ministry.

God had given me several dreams showing the lights going out in the church. God showed the ministry's spiritual climate, the demons that were active in the church, and the inaccurate prophetic words that were being delivered in the service. Then God showed me the minister falling and hitting his head. I spoke to the minister regarding the dreams. He thought the dreams were about me, dismissed the revelation, and began to minister to me, believing the dreams were an indication of my spiritual shortcomings. Naturally, there was a resistance to sharing everything God was showing me with my pastor and mentor. I actually started doubting my interpretation of the dreams. I realized it was hard for a seasoned minister and prophet to hear God speaking through someone that was immature as a Christian and had not been developed as a prophet. Finally, God gave me a dream showing me under another ministry, but I did not leave because of loyalty to my pastor. Then God stopped speaking. I realized my fault and moved immediately. God has been speaking to me ever since.

WHY CAN'T I HEAR YOU, GOD?

When God seems to be quiet and not speaking to you, ask yourself:

- What was the last revelation you received? What did God say to you?
- Did He ask you to do something? Did you do it?
- Did He ask you to go somewhere? Did you go?
- Did He ask you to pray for someone? Did you pray?

God is silent for a reason. Ask Him why. God will respond.

GOD IS SPEAKING

God speaks in various ways. God can talk through:

- Dreams (Joel 2:28–29);
- Visions (Acts 10);
- Direct audible speech (John 12:28–29);
- Scripture (Psalm 119:105);
- A still small voice (1 Kings 19:12);
- Gifts of the Holy Spirit—wisdom, knowledge, prophecy (1 Corinthians 12:8, 10);
- Natural circumstances, such as words on a church marque or a billboard;
- People, such as intercessors and prayer partners.

As you can see from the list above, God speaks to us in many ways.

EIGHT PURPOSES OF DREAMS, VISIONS, AND REVELATIONS

1. God reveals His heart, will, and mysteries to us in the night. (Job 33:14, AMP)
2. God awakens our desire to walk and interact with Him.

3. God imparts intercessory burdens for us to pray for people, places, and things.
4. God entrusts us with secrets, inventions, or instructions.
5. God reveals visions of future events to warn, predict, or give strategic guidance.
6. God reveals our destiny or callings.
7. God releases revelation (natural or supernatural) to awaken our spirit.
8. God wants to bring healing and deliverance to people, cities, nations, and the land.

DREAMS

In her book *Revelatory Encounters,* Barbie Breathitt reveals the many ways God communicates: intuition, inner knowledge, pictures, logos word, rhema word, visions, internal/external/open visions, dreams, trances, visitations, fire, lightning, thunder, wind, and audible voice.

One of the most common methods God uses to communicate is through dreams. There are many examples of God speaking through dreams in the Bible. In Genesis 20:3, 6, God warned Abimelech (a pagan king) in a dream concerning Abraham's wife, Sarah. In Genesis 40:8–19, God gave Joseph the interpretation of the chief cupbearer and the chief baker's dreams. In Daniel 2:1–49, God revealed the understanding of the pagan Persian King Nebuchadnezzar's dream to Daniel.

In Numbers 12:6–7, God said, "Listen to my words: 'When a prophet of the LORD is among you, I reveal myself to him in visions. I speak to him in dreams.'"

In Matthew 1:18–21, 24, 25, God spoke through an angel to Joseph through a dream concerning Mary's pregnancy. In Matthew 2:12, the Magi were warned in a dream not to return to King Herod. In Matthew 2:13, the Lord told Joseph in a dream to take Mary and Jesus to escape to Egypt and remain in Egypt until the Lord told them to return. In Matthew 2:19–23, an angel of the Lord appeared in a dream to Joseph in Egypt and told him to return to Israel. He took his family and moved to Nazareth, so was fulfilled the prophecy that Jesus would be called a Nazarene.

TYPES OF DREAMS

There are three basic types of dreams:

1. Simple—there is no need for interpretation. The dream is direct and to the point. Such as the Magi's dream in Matthew 2:12 when they were told not to return to King Herod. And Joseph's dream in Matthew 2:13 when he was told to go and take his family to Egypt because King Herod was going to search for Jesus to kill him.
2. Simple symbolic dream—the dreamer understands the symbolism in the dream; thus, it is easily understood by the dreamer. In Genesis 37:5–11, Joseph told his dream to his brothers and father. They immediately understood the symbolism of the dream and its interpretation.

3. Complex dreams—the symbolism contains a hidden message that is not easily understood by the dreamer. In Daniel 2, King Nebuchadnezzar had a dream about a tree that was cut down. The King commanded the magicians, enchanters, sorcerers, and astrologers to tell him what he dreamed and what it meant. None of them could do what the king commanded, so he ordered his army's commander to put them to death. When Daniel was told he went to the king to ask for time to pray about the king's dream. God answered Daniel's prayer. Daniel gave God the glory before he told the king the dream and its interpretation. Read Daniel 4 to see the king's response.

There are two main categories of dreams:

1. Intrinsic—these are personal dreams about the dreamer in which the dreamer is a participant

in the dream. About 80–90% of dreams are personal dreams.

2. Extrinsic—these are external dreams where the dreamer is an observer of an event related to the dreamer's sphere of authority (family, friends, work, church, city, nation, etc.). The most common purposes of external dreams are to draw the dreamer into an assignment requiring action or into intercession. Even if it is an assignment, intercession should be first!

As you can see from the list above, God reveals many things to us in dreams, visions, and revelations. We must rely on God to clearly define why He has given the revelation. The Spirit of truth will guide you in all the truth. (John 16:13)

God gives us revelation to bring about His will on earth. It is essential to remain humble and be a good steward of the revelation God has given you. There will be times you do not know what to do with the revelation. There are other times when you will want to share it with others and receive confirmation that you heard from God.

WHAT IS GOD SAYING?

Have you ever had a dream that you know is an important dream and promised yourself to write it down in the morning, and when morning came, you could not remember the dream? I have. After this happened to me a few times, I learned it is good to keep a pen and paper next to the bed to immediately write down the dream. By writing key pieces of the dream, I knew I would remember the dream. Then, I could add the details in the morning.

Keep in mind, God is the revealer of all dreams and mysteries. During the interpretation process, we must rely on the Holy Spirit for all revelation.

There are three sources of dreams: God, the human soul/desires, and the devil. Even when the dream is not from God, the Holy Spirit can reveal the dream's origin.

When you dream, you may immediately know the interpretation of the dream. If so, be sure to take appropriate action in response to what God is saying to you.

If you do not understand the meaning of the dream, pray, and ask God what it means. He may not respond immediately. You may have to fast, pray, and search out the meaning using the Bible and dream interpretation books.

There are many books on dream interpretation on the market. I recommend purchasing a Bible-based book rather than one written by psychics or secular authors. The three Christian based dream interpretation books I use most often are:

1. *When God Speaks*, by Chuck D. Pierce and Rebecca Wagner Sytsema;
2. *Dream Encounters, Seeing Your Destiny from God's Perspective*, by Barbie L. Breathitt; and
3. *Divinity Code to Understanding Your Dreams and Visions*, by Adam F. Thompson and Adrian Beale.

These books offer practical guidance on how to understand God's symbolic dream language and interpret dream revelation. God uses numbers; colors; creatures; things such as cars, buses, airplanes, buildings; people symbols, such as father, baby, governor, bride; and symbols that pertain to nature, weather, and natural elements (fire, water, wind) to communicate with us through dreams and visions. When you believe you understand the dream, pray, and ask God if your interpretation is correct and complete.

At times, we think we understand what God is saying, but we want additional confirmation from God. Often, God will confirm the dream's interpretation through natural circumstances, such as words spoken in a church service, or through television shows or movies, or a person you know. Our ears perk up when we hear the confirmation, and we know we correctly understood the dream's interpretation.

As we pursue an interpretation, we can ask specific questions that help gain revelation over the dream or vision. The following questions were taken from *When*

God Speaks, by Chuck D. Pierce and Rebecca Wagner Sytsema, page 82:

- To whom does the dream refer?
- What is it really about?
- What is the setting(s)?
- What is the symbolism in the dream?
- What are the current circumstances and history of the one who received the dream or vision?
- What is God's timing in fulfilling the dream or vision? (Ask this question once there is a handle on the interpretation.)
- Based on the dream, what responsibility does the one who received the dream or vision have?

God speaks to us through dreams and visions for a reason. Ask God to help you to learn to know His voice. Pray for a teachable spirit. Listen when God speaks with the intent to obey God. Call to God, and He will answer (Jeremiah 33:3). God wants to communicate with you!

Section Four

Heart of Worship Opens Windows of Heaven

My tongue will proclaim Your righteousness,
Your praises all day long. (Psalm 35:28)

IN THE INTRODUCTION TO THIS BOOK, I listed four outcomes you can expect from reading this book. One is when you call to God, He will answer you. The following two scriptures from the Bible lay a great foundation to achieve this objective: "If you seek the Lord, you will find him if you seek Him with all of your heart and with all of your soul" (Deuteronomy 4:29). "Love the Lord your God with all your heart and with all your soul and with all your strength" (Deuteronomy 6:5).

These scriptures tell you to seek God and love God with all your heart and all your soul. You may ask, How do I seek and love the Lord with all my heart and soul? An excellent way to start is through praise and worship. Similar to you telling your family and friends you love them, tell the Lord you love Him. Or just like you invite your friends and family into your home because you want to spend time with them, and create memories of the time you share, ask the Lord into your home and your heart. Spend time with Him. Think about Him throughout the day, in the same way as you would your family, friends, or pets.

Ask yourself, do you love the Lord as much as you love your family, your friends, and your pets? Do you look forward to spending time with Him at the end of your work/school day as much as you do with your family, your friends, and your pets? Is your heart filled with joy when you think about the Lord? As much joy as when you think about your family, your friends, or your pets? Are you sad when you come home and find the Lord is not there?

What is your heart telling you? In the depth of your soul, what are you hearing? Your response to these questions will provide you with insight into whether you seek the Lord and love Him with all your heart. The good news is God loves you no matter how you responded to these questions.

God patiently waits for you to love Him. You can invite Him into your heart today, and He will rejoice and joyfully spend time with you! *God is eager to spend time with you!*

WORSHIP THE LORD IN SPIRIT AND TRUTH

When you worship God in spirit and truth, He will answer you. King David was a mighty warrior. He understood the importance of praise and worship. He is known for his psalms of praise and worship to God. God described David as "my servant David, who kept

My commands and followed Me with all his heart, doing only what was right in My eyes" (1 Kings 14:8).

When King David returned the Ark of the Covenant to Jerusalem, he "was dancing before the LORD with all his might, while he and all Israel were bringing up the ark of the LORD with shouts and the sound of trumpets... King David was 'leaping and dancing before the LORD'" (2 Samuel 6:14–16).

King David loved God and had a heart of worship. He wrote many of the psalms of praise found throughout the Bible. "God is enthroned upon the praises of His people" (Psalm 22:3, NASB,) and from that throne, God hears and answers our prayers.

Heartfelt worship and praise reach the throne of Heaven. God delights in our sincere praises. At times, when we praise, our heart is not focused on God. Our mind is someplace else. Our worship may be affected by distractions. We may sing the songs, but the melodies do not touch our hearts. We may not experience the joy and peace that comes from praising God.

Heart of Worship Opens Windows of Heaven

We all experience trials and tribulations throughout our lives. It is during these times; some of us find it challenging to connect with God. If this happens, call to God with a heart of worship. Do your best to:

- Set a guard over your mouth;
- Only believe—do not speak or pray in unbelief;
- Speak God's Word into the atmosphere;
- Trust God—God watches over His Word to perform it;
- Choose to walk in God's blessings;
- Choose to go God's way—walk the path God has for you;
- Shout to God with a voice of triumph!

Meditate on God's Word day and night, so you may be careful to do everything written in it. Ask God to give you strategies for prophetic intercession.

Prayers and intercession for others can have a life-changing impact on people, nations, and kingdoms. Intercessory prayer is biblical. See 1 Timothy 2:1–2;

James 5:13–16; Ephesians 6:10–20; Matthew 21:22. God's methods of responding will vary. One person may receive a mental impression, and another may receive a dream, another may hear His voice speaking through their surroundings. As noted above, God speaks in various ways. In Ephesians 6:18, we read, "Pray in the Spirit on all occasions with all kinds of prayers and requests. With this in mind, be alert and always keep on praying for all the Lord's people."

Our prayers are mighty weapons that have divine power to demolish strongholds, arguments, and every pretension that sets itself up against the knowledge of God (2 Corinthians 10:4–5).

- Pray every day.
- Keep your momentum going until you achieve a breakthrough.
- Fervently intercede in faith, expecting the situation to change.
- Pray prayers of adoration and love to God in addition to prayers for a specific need.

God created us to worship and praise Him. He wants to help us fight our battles. He wants us to pray and stand in faith with others who are fighting battles.

HEART OF GRACE

Have you ever seen a caller's name show up on your phone and thought, "I do not want to take this call; this caller will spend hours talking about the caller's spouse, children, job, or other problems the caller is going through. I do not want to deal with this today"? Or have you ever had a neighbor or family member or friend drop by your house and you pretended you were not home?

Maybe you have not, but I have. I can remember, many years ago, a childhood friend would stop by my house to visit with her six kids. I reasoned with myself that I did not want to invite her in because our conversations were constantly interrupted by her kids, who were always getting into something. What I did not know at the time is she was in an abusive marriage. She was coming to visit to seek refuge from a tumultuous home. All I could think about was my selfish desire to have time to spend with me and my friend without her kids.

That was when I did not have a heart of grace. That was when I arrogantly thought, "I do not have the time or energy to listen to people who have a lot of problems or deal with my friend who had a lot of kids." How sad. Even now, when I think about it, it makes me confess and repent again for my selfish, arrogant attitude.

When I reflect on who I was then and who I am now, I honestly believe someone who knew me was interceding for me—praying for my heart to change. I am thankful others stood before God on my behalf so I can stand in the gap on behalf of others. It takes a heart of grace to care enough about others to pray for them. A spirit of mercy enables us to go before God to seek His guidance to help others.

Through a heart of grace, we can walk alongside those being held captive by addictions, poverty, delusions, violent actions of others, sexual immorality, human trafficking, or any other force of evil, and intercede for them to be set free. God wants us to extend grace to others, just like God extends grace to all humanity. Our intercessory prayers for others are an example of how to express our heart of grace.

SPIRITUAL HEARING TO INTERCEDE

God may be speaking to you because He wants you to pray and intercede for a person, place, or nation. Prayer is an appeal to God to intervene in a situation. Prayers do not have to be lengthy. Merely praying, "God help me," will arouse a response from God. If you do not know how to pray, ask God how to pray. Be ready to receive a new way of thinking about what concerns you when God gives you a new level of understanding of how to pray for yourself or others. If you listen with an open heart, you will receive more revelation (Mark 4:25).

Understanding the times and seasons is vital to interpret the world around you. In Ecclesiastes, we read, "There is a time for everything and a season for every activity under the heavens." "A time to tear down and a time to build, a time to be silent and a time to speak" (Ecclesiastes 3:1, 7). This understanding helps you to know when to speak the appropriate words at the right time.

Stay alert and attuned to the revelation God is speaking now. It is easy to slip into rote intercession. Rote intercession is a prayer of scripture that is out of time. Yes, it is a scripture, but it is out of time—it has the word without the Spirit. An example of rote intercession is praying prayers that are clichés or taken verbatim from prayer books. Please understand, I am not saying prayer books are not excellent tools that provide scriptures for prayers; they are. However, they should not be a substitute for seeking God and listening to what He is saying for the situation or person.

At times, strategic prayer networks use rote intercession. They dispatch intercessors to pray a specific, repetitive prewritten prayer at every prayer site. As in the case of using prayer books, this interceding method for God to change a territory impedes the intercessors from listening to what God is saying. The revelation

God released in one season may not apply to the current season.

Another example of rote intercession are prayers for healing. The prayer may have resulted in recovery for one individual but not worked for someone else. Praying a list of scriptures that pertain to healing or any other prayer need will, at times, result in a positive change but not always.

The holy word of God is powerful—God wants us to pray His word in reverence, not as though it is a magic formula.

When we do not know how to pray, God wants us to seek Him for guidance on how to pray. God may give a word of knowledge concerning the underlying cause of the prayer need. When He does, trust you hear from God and pray the prayers He wants to be prayed when He wants them prayed. Prayers released in God's timing get results.

STAND IN THE GAP—STRATEGIC PROPHETIC INTERCESSION

So, I sought for a man among them who would make a wall and stand in the gap before Me on behalf of the land, that I should not destroy it; but I found no one.
Ezekiel 22:30

Strategic prophetic intercession penetrates the atmosphere to establish God's will on earth as it is in Heaven. It may require fasting, in addition to praying and inquiring of the Lord to hear His will for a given situation. These appeals to Heaven include speaking prophetic declarations by declaring God's words in response to your prayers and worship over specific problems.

The purpose of strategic prophetic intercession is to take us into the throne room of God as intercessors during our passionate, heartfelt worship to effect changes in a situation to align it with God's will.

Strategic prophetic intercession is similar to apostolic worship discussed in *Worship as It Is in Heaven,* by John Dickson and Chuck Pierce. Their book describes the impact apostolic worship has on corporate settings over specific problems and warfare areas in a community, city, region, state, or nation.

"Apostolic worship is worship that facilitates the government of God as He enthrones Himself on our praises. It is worship that brings us into the Lord's governmental process on the earth as it is in Heaven" (Ibid, pages 24, 25).

Chuck Pierce says this:

> Most Christians focus their worship on relationship and adoration, which is both excellent and right. However, our adoration and quest to know God must also move to a higher level—that of exercising His will on earth. What God is doing and saying in Heaven must be manifested on earth. As we worship, our

> adoration ascends to His throne. It is through this process that we are able to then descend in effective warfare (Ibid, page 35).

Strategic prophetic intercession is a higher level of intercession combined with worship. It is ascending into Heaven as warriors of God to effect changes that will bring about God's will on earth. Through our praise, worship, prophetic utterances, declarations, and decrees, we change the atmosphere. As we break out of old prayer and worship cycles and listen to what the Holy Spirit is saying, we can change the situation and bring about God's will.

Strategic prophetic intercession and apostolic worship will release revelation from God. Revelation is similar to a flowing river. Some ministers use the term "the river of God" as a metaphor for revelation. Holy Spirit is often symbolically referred to as a river. In John 7:38, 39, Jesus said,

He who believes in Me, as the Scripture said, "From his innermost being will flow rivers of living water." By this He spoke of the Spirit, whom those who believed in Him were to receive for the Spirit was not yet given because Jesus was not yet glorified.

In Revelation 22:1, an angel showed the Apostle John "the river of water of life as clear as crystal, flowing from the throne of God and of the Lamb."

RIVERS OF LIVING WATER

"There is a river whose streams make glad the city of God, the holy place where the Most High dwells." (Psalm 46:4)

All true revelation comes from God the Father, God the Son, and God the Holy Spirit. The above scripture tells us God is in the midst of the river; the river of life flows from the throne of God and of the Lamb; and, within our innermost being "flow rivers of living water," which is the Holy Spirit of God who dwells within us.

Our internal river is like a river in the natural that is replenished by rains that give it height causing rivulets (brooks, creeks, and streams) to flow throughout the land. As the rivulets of living water flow within our body, soul, and spirit, we receive divine revelation and strategies from Heaven to destroy the works of the devil and advance the Kingdom of God.

Just as rivers need replenishing to keep from running dry, so does our relationship with God. Sometimes when we take Him for granted and pay more attention to our needs, interests, and desires, our brooks begin to run dry. Even though our living water level is dropping and our creeks are drying up, we may not notice it at first.

We may stop receiving dreams and visions from God. Our revelatory gifts, prophecy, word of knowledge, or word of wisdom may begin to diminish. Our river might become dangerously low before we notice, or the riverbed may go completely dry. Like a riverbed during a drought, it needs more water. We may need to dig deep within our souls during these times to break forth a new wellspring.

IN PURSUIT OF GOD'S PRESENCE

There is an eternal source of living water within us that is always available for us to tap into—the Holy Spirit never leaves. Although we may not feel His presence, God is still in our midst. He is ever-present. He is deep within our innermost being—we may need to drill deep through the hardness of our heart that we have developed over time to tap into His revitalizing living water.

As we drill deeper (demonstrated through our intercessory prayers and worship), we can tap into God's "River of Delights." God's unfailing love is always available to us. He provides us refuge and a fountain of life. In Psalms 36:7, 8, we read: "How priceless is your unfailing love, O God! People take refuge in the shadow of your wings. They feast on the abundance of your house; you give them drink from your river of delights. For with you is the fountain of life; in your light, we see the light."

God's river of delights is like a tsunami. It is a powerful river of living water that will gush out as we worship and praise God and bring forth cleansing and healing for our drought-ridden souls. Doubt, anger, and unforgiveness create communication barriers between God and us.

God's river of living water breaks through barriers to communicating with God that may have been built by unbelief, doubt, anger, or unforgiveness. It flows with fresh, pure, holy water. It releases new, pure, holy revelation. It will reveal areas in your life when you did not believe God was with you or when you doubted God would hear and answer your prayers. Possibly you are angry with God because a loved one died.

God's river of living water will flush out the bitterness and cleanse you of the anger which you allowed to take root in your soul and spirit because of unforgiveness. It will wash away every impediment, which is blocking your two-way communications with God.

The river of God flows from Heaven onto people and penetrates their minds, spirits, and souls, absorbing them, and filling them with righteousness, holiness, pure revelation, wisdom, knowledge, understanding, and reverent, loving fear of God.

God invites all humanity to walk in the overflow of His power and enjoy His living river. In John 7:38, Lord Jesus said, "Whoever believes in me, as Scripture has said, rivers of living water will flow from within them." By this, the Lord meant the Holy Spirit, whom those who believe in the Lord Jesus receive. The Lord promises we will be abundantly satisfied as we drink from the river of the Lord's pleasures. (Psalms 36:8 NKJV)

Strategic prophetic intercession and apostolic worship can help us to break into wellsprings we have yet to discover. Waters clear as crystal flowing from the throne of God and of the Lamb are within us still untapped, waiting to burst forth into a new, fresh flow of the Spirit.

When we break through, the water rushes to the surface and refills our dry riverbed and rivulets afresh and anew.

Praise and worship fine-tune our spiritual ears to hear at a deeper level than we heard before with greater clarity and accuracy. Our worship will take us into new realms of revelation to discern the heart of God. We will hear what God is saying and what He is doing in the Spirit. God will release new strategies, open new doors, and reveal new opportunities to accomplish His will on earth as it is in Heaven. Our pursuit of God's Presence will be successful. We will ascend in worship and descend in revelation!

THE DOOR IS OPEN

The foundation or praise and worship opens the door to "Call to the Lord so He will answer you" (Jeremiah 33:3). The Lord God wants us to love Him with all our heart, soul, and strength. God wants to commune with us daily. He wants to have an eternal relationship with us.

Each one of us has access to a life of eternity in Heaven with God. If we confess His Son, Jesus Christ, is Lord and believe in our heart that God raised Him from the dead, we receive eternal salvation. For it is with our heart we believe and are justified, and it is with our mouth, we profess our faith and are saved. God has given us eternal life, and this life is in His Son. Everyone who has the Son has life, and everyone who does not have the Son does not have eternal life (Romans 10:9, 10; 1 John 5:11, 12).

Salvation is a gift from God. Although God offers the gift of salvation to everyone, God gives each person the ability to choose to receive His gift. A person does not have to accept the gift of salvation to call to God. He will answer, even when the person is not saved.

God is a loving God and the Creator of all humanity. He wants to hear from us, all of us. God hears and answers the prayers of both those who confess Jesus Christ, God's Son is Lord, and those who do not. However, the only way to spend eternity with God the Father and the Lord Jesus Christ is to confess Lord

Jesus is your Lord. A prayer for salvation is at the end of this chapter.

MADE TO RULE

God created humans to rule over His creation. Our authority over the earth depends on our willingness to submit to, serve, and obey the living God who holds sovereign power over all creation. We are intrinsically distinct from the rest of creation; the Lord has given us dominion over the earth and everything upon it (Psalm 8:6 NKJV).

We are the gatekeepers God has put in place in our regions, for God marked out our appointed times in history and the boundaries of our lands (Acts 17:26). God destined us to rule in our regions before the beginning of time. God created us to be God's ambassadors on earth. As delegated rulers on this earth, we have a responsibility to understand the times.

Lord Jesus spoke clearly about interpreting the world around us. In Luke 12:56, Jesus said,

"Hypocrites! You know how to interpret the appearance of the earth and the sky. How is it that you do not know how to interpret this present time?" Also, in Matthew 16:3, Jesus said, "You know how to interpret the appearance of the sky, but you cannot interpret the signs of the times."

Jesus revealed to us we must know what is going on around us. We must understand and learn how to interpret the present time in the world around us.

In the book *Interpreting the Times: How God intersects with our lives to bring revelation and understanding*, by Chuck D. Pierce, he challenges his readers to ponder the following questions:

- Does time control you?
- Do you understand how to maneuver through societal change and not allow those changes to overtake you?
- Do you feel manipulated or captured by time?
- Does time seem to be your enemy?

- Does your past control your present and leave you confused about your future?
- Do you believe you have a future that is good?

One primary focus of this book is to teach us when we mess up in one season, God can make us capable of redeeming the time. By faith, we can transition from one season into another and successfully crossover into a new dimension of success.

We do not have to allow our past to dictate our future. Lord Jesus came to earth to offer the gift of salvation. We can redeem the time and not let our past mistakes dictate our future. Lord Jesus came so we can have and enjoy life and have it in abundance (John 10:10).

For God loved the world so much, He gave His one and only Son as a gift. So now, everyone who believes in His Son will never perish but experience everlasting life (John 3:16). If you have not accepted Lord Jesus Christ as your savior, now is a great time to leave your past behind and choose God's gift of salvation.

SALVATION PRAYER

Heavenly Father, it is written in Your Holy Word that if I confess with my mouth that Jesus is Lord and I believe in my heart that You raised Jesus from the dead, then I shall be saved. Father, I confess that Jesus is my Lord. I make Jesus Lord of my life right now. I believe in my heart that You raised Your Son, Jesus, from the dead. I renounce my past life with Satan and close the door to all his devices. I thank You for forgiving me of all my sins and for saving me. I declare Jesus is my Lord. In the name of Jesus, I pray. Amen. (Romans 10:9)

Section Five

God Speaks—Interpreting the World Around You

> *For God does speak—now one way, now another—though no one perceives it. In a dream, in a vision of the night, when deep sleep falls on people as they slumber in their beds, then He opens their ears and seals their instruction.* (Job 33:14-16, NIV, NKJV)

JUST AS GOD SPOKE TO JOSEPH IN A dream instructing him to flee to Egypt with Mary and baby Jesus, God still speaks in dreams today (Matthew 2:13).

A New Era of Prophecy Prepare to Listen!

A few years ago, I had a dream. In the dream, my father called me and asked me if I had his phone or if I had seen his phone. I told him no. I was glad to hear from him, but I was busy cleaning my house. My floors were dirty; they were new tile floors that needed cleaning. I had poured too much water on the floor, and I was trying to mop it quickly to keep it from going all over the place. Suddenly, my father appeared. He asked me again about his phone. He wanted me to go with him. I was trying to mop up the wet floor. He asked me again to come with him, and I went.

In the next scene in the dream, my father and I were in horizontal tubes, shooting forth—he was in one, I was in one next to him. We were shooting through enemies and destroying them. We were the weapons. As we shot through the tube, we destroyed the enemies. When we shot out of the tubes, we were at a place where there was a large, tall structure, similar to a large missile. It was at the core of the room. We were in a position to destroy it. I woke up, but I knew we would destroy it.

When I awoke, my interpretation of the dream was: My father was God. The phone He was asking about was His phone but also my phone. We had a family plan network, so when He calls, I have a direct line to His phone. He wanted me to know we had a direct line between us. When He came, I was too busy with chores (mopping) to stop and give Him my full attention. I felt I had to finish what I was doing. God wants us to stop and listen when He calls. At times, when we are troubled about something, we pray and then busy ourselves trying to work through the issue on our own. God wants us to know He is alongside us during our battles. Together, we will identify and conquer the core issue.

Four days after I had that dream, a prophetic word was spoken by Chuck Pierce during Sunday morning service in which he said, "God will shoot you forth, and you will target not only what He wants you to target, but the enemy who has been targeting you." I thought, Wow! God confirmed His dream.

I believe this dream is for us all. God is saying, "Come and go with Me." By His power and might, together, we will destroy our enemies—fear, anxieties, unbelief—anything hindering our progress. The enemy cannot stand against God's power. When we co-labor with God, the enemy cannot hold us back. We will destroy the enemy and get to the core, the root cause.

ROOT CAUSE ANALYSIS

Often prayers focus on the symptom without getting to the root. Much time and effort go into addressing the surface of an issue without getting to the root cause. Prayers that target the problem with pinpoint accuracy get results.

Before praying over a matter of concern, ask the Lord how to pray. Listen. What word or words come to mind? Write the words down. Search for scriptures containing each keyword to learn what is written about your concern. If you have multiple translations of the Bible on your computer or phone, search each version for the keyword. The keyword may be found in the KJV and not in NIV or another translation. The keyword may be in modern translations, such as the AMP, MSG, or TPT translation. The word may not be the same word used in older translations. After you complete your word search, meditate on the scriptures that speak to your heart. Hear what God is saying. Allow God to reveal the root of the issue.

Conducting a root cause analysis is a standard analytical tool used in businesses to go beyond a surface examination of problems or issues. Many problems can be solved using this systematic approach.

An example of a root cause analysis is shown below. By spending time to probe the following six levels of the problem by asking, "Why is that?" to analyze the situation, we can pray targeted prayers and apply our Kingdom authority to the real issues and see change occur.

ROOT CAUSE ANALYSIS— HOW DOES GOD SEE IT?	
How would you describe the problem?	How would you describe how God sees the problem?
Why is that?	Why is that?
On the surface, how would you describe your basic assumptions as to why this problem is occurring?	How would you say God would describe your basic assumptions as to why the problem is occurring?
Why is that?	Why is that?
Who are the people directly or indirectly involved in this problem? What is the consistent behavior they exhibit when this problem occurs?	How would you say God would describe the people's consistent behavior directly or indirectly when this problem occurs?
Why is that?	Why is that?

God Speaks—Interpreting the World Around You

What controllable factors influence the people involved in this problem? What uncontrollable factors influence them?	What would you say God would state as the controllable and uncontrollable factors that influence the people involved in this problem?
Why is that?	Why is that?
What would you describe as the habit, tradition, or obligation connected to this problem?	What would you say God would say is the habit, tradition, or obligation connected to this problem?
Why is that?	Why is that?
What do you see as the solution?	What does God see as the solution?
Why is that?	Why is that?

Taking time to complete the root cause analysis above will provide constructive, thought-provoking insight into the problem. You will focus on your ideas about the situation and seek the Lord to hear His thoughts concerning the matter (Jeremiah 33:3).

Many people, at some time during their lives, experience an identity crisis. They conduct an internal analysis to find a meaning for their lives. They question who they are, why they are here, their purpose, and their calling—they wrestle with questions about their true identity.

Rather than relying only on their thoughts, they will better understand their purpose and calling when they also ask God. As they ask the questions in the root cause analysis mentioned above, they begin to discover who they are and their passions as God reveals His responses to them.

Following is an example root cause analysis using the questions found in the chart above:

What do I see as my emotional expression of the problem that is immediately identifiable? I feel frustrated because I am not fulfilling the plans I have for my life.

Why is that? Because I am not satisfied with doing what I am doing. I know I can do more.

How would you describe the problem? I do not like the job I have.

Why is that? It is not rewarding.

On the surface, how would you describe your basic assumptions as to why this problem is occurring? I am not able to fully use my knowledge, skills, abilities, and talents.

Why is that? My boss does not welcome or want my input concerning the job.

Who are the people directly or indirectly involved in this problem? What is the consistent behavior they exhibit when this problem occurs? My boss. My boss does not listen to me when I try to offer creative ideas for doing the job.

Why is that? The company culture does not welcome input from its workers.

What controllable factors influence the people involved in this problem? What uncontrollable factors influence them? My boss has the authority to make changes but has worked at the same company for over 20 years and is not open to new ideas.

Why is that? The company culture is not a culture that values change.

What habit, tradition, or obligation is connected to this problem? It is a decades-old business with long-term leaders and outdated company policies and work rules.

Why is that? The company leaders are resistant to change.

What do you see as the solution? Changing jobs, but I am afraid to quit.

Why is that? Because I want to start my own business, but I do not have the faith to believe I can do it.

Now, let's ask the same questions from the perspective of how God sees it.

What do I see as God's view of my emotional expression of the problem that is immediately identifiable? He longs for me to seek Him—to ask Him why I feel like I am not fulfilling my plans for my life.

Why is that? Because He knows the plans He has for me, plans to prosper me and not harm me, plans to give me hope and a future (Jeremiah 29:11).

How would you describe how God sees the problem? He would say the job I am in does not allow me to be the person He created me to be.

Why is that? Because He created my inmost being. He knit me together in my mother's womb (Psalm 139:13). He knows this job does not allow me to use my creation gifts and express my true identity and fulfill the plans He has for my future.

On the surface, how would God describe your basic assumptions as to why this problem is occurring? He would say, "Do not fear or be discouraged." Although I am in a job where I cannot fully utilize my knowledge, skills, abilities, and talents, He will help me get to the place He has chosen for me to go to do the things He created me to do (Deut. 1:21).

Why is that? There is an appointed time for everything. There is a time for every purpose under the heavens (Eccl. 3:1). God blessed me with this job to prepare my heart for the purpose and plans He has for me.

How would you say God would describe the people's consistent behavior directly or indirectly when this problem occurs? He would say, He knows the plans He has for them. If they seek Him with all their heart, they will find Him and become the leaders He destined them to be (Jeremiah 29:11–13).

Why is that? Because God is love. He wants the best for everyone.

What would you say God would say are the controllable and uncontrollable factors that influence the people involved in this problem? Although they cannot control every factor that affects them, He would say if they seek Him and lead with integrity, He will guide them.

Why is that? Although the company culture is not a culture that seems to value change, God would say, "Righteousness guards the person of integrity" (Proverbs 13:6).

What would you say God would say is a habit, tradition, or obligation connected to this problem? Their culture of integrity has sustained them and made them a decades-old business. If they continue to seek the Lord to learn His plans for their business, He will answer them and tell them great and unsearchable things they do not know (Jeremiah 33:3).

Why is that? Because God uses others to teach and prepare us for the future.

What does God see as the solution? Fear not! Trust God. He will establish the works of my hands. He wants me to commit my plans to Him, and they will succeed (Psalm 90:17; Proverbs 16:3).

Why is that? Because God did not give me a spirit of fear but of power and love and a sound mind (2 Timothy 1:7 NKJV).

The Bible makes it clear God has a purpose and a plan for our lives. But if we do not seek God, it is hard to discern what that plan is. In the Bible, when someone wanted to know the will of God, they "inquired of the Lord," meaning they asked Him, and He told them.

It is just as important to "inquire of the Lord" today as it was during biblical times. God continually reveals new revelations. He is frequently speaking to His people. When we meditate on God's Word and seek Him, He is faithful to give us the strategies we need to succeed. God is speaking. He wants us to listen!

BREAKING BARRIERS TO UNANSWERED PRAYER

Stereotypes affect how we treat others. We must remove our blinders and biases to express a heart of grace for others. Our preferences and prejudices will not only affect how we interact with others—they can also affect how we pray for them.

Judgment and biases can also influence how we pray and how we hear God's voice. Ask God to remove all of your thoughts on what you think God should do to bring about change. Listen to what God has to say concerning the situation. Ask yourself, "Is my solution really what God wants?" Ask yourself, "Do my desires line up in spirit and truth with the Word of God?"

Is it possible you are praying the desires of your heart, rather than the desires of God's heart? For example, are you praying for God to change someone according to how you want that person to act or behave? Or are you submitting the person to God and trusting God for His solution? Possibly God has some work to do in you both to get you aligned to His purposes and plans. Always strive to listen to hear what God is saying about the situation. Open your ears and heart to hear God.

It can be easy to slip into your thoughts or explanations for another person's behavior and miss the spiritual stronghold the person has allowed to set up and establish roots in the person's mind. Strongholds block clarity of thinking.

STRONGHOLDS EXPOSED

Ed Silvoso, president of Harvest Evangelism, defines a spiritual stronghold as "a mindset impregnated with hopelessness that leads us to accept as unchangeable situations that we know are contrary to the will of God." According to him, spiritual strongholds are built in the "mind by Satan so he can manipulate behavior without being detected." (Ed Silvoso, *That None Should Perish*, Ventura, California: Regal Books, 1994)

Spiritual strongholds can result from coming into agreement with a lie. They can hinder a person from walking into the destiny God has for that person. And they can stop a person from taking a stand for God for fear they will be viewed negatively by society. Spiritual strongholds must be overcome in one's mind before that person can demolish the stronghold.

METHODS TO BREAK STRONGHOLDS

Methods to break strongholds and see changes come are:

- Challenge your thinking process—get rid of old mindsets;
- Question your desires—the lusts of your heart and eyes;
- Google "promises of God in the Bible"—meditate on and believe God's promises;

- As you meditate on the Bible, hear, listen, and obey the voice of God.

Spiritual strongholds are deceptive; you may not always recognize a spiritual stronghold. Dishonesty, betrayal, fraud, corruption, and cheating all involve deliberate concealment, distortions, or misrepresentations. These strongholds can cause a person to believe something that is not true and lead that person into error, danger, despair, or a disadvantageous position.

Manipulative behavior, another stronghold, can be accomplished by pleasant, alluring methods or outright lies. Unknowingly we can let false perceptions control our beliefs about ourselves and the world around us. Although these deceptive thoughts and feelings are wrong, they still have power.

Ask God to reveal any strongholds you have so you can do what God tells you to do to overcome and destroy its grip. God wants you, your family, and your friends free from strongholds. Pray for God to teach you how to be victorious. Invite God to show you how to mind your mind!

MIND CONTROL—MIND YOUR MIND

Mind control techniques used by the media can slowly change the way you think when you are not firmly rooted in your beliefs. The changes in culture during the past 30 years since the introduction of the Internet are evidence of the impact media has on belief systems.

An example of this can be found in the "fake news" reported by the media or the Internet. Fake news is a term attributed to deliberate outright lies published to misrepresent facts or to mislead others. It is not the same as sloppy or immature journalism—it is intentional.

Fake news is purposeful. It is distributed to manipulate how a person thinks. Renowned newscasters, editors, and writers have lost their jobs for publishing articles or broadcasting fake news. Some commentators maintain the false stories published in newspapers, magazines, and the Internet affected the 2016 and 2020

US presidential elections. Fake news can have a powerful, worldwide impact.

Social media intentionally targets your emotions to influence how you think and react by glamorizing sinful behavior and condemning righteous behavior. "Those who are motivated by the flesh only pursue what benefits themselves. But those who live by the impulses of the Holy Spirit are motivated to pursue spiritual realities. For the mindset of the flesh is death, but the mindset controlled by the Spirit finds life and peace. In fact, the mindset focused on the flesh fights God's plan and refuses to submit to his direction" (Romans 8:5–7, TPT).

Society is bombarded daily with words and images that impact the way we think and make decisions. It is said, "Our perceptions are our reality." Our views shape who we are because of what we allow ourselves to think or believe, so it is vital to guard our minds.

Considering the magnitude of fake news broadcast via the news and social media, now more than ever is the time to seek God and earnestly desire to be close to God to hear and discern His voice accurately.

When faced with a difficult decision, be careful how you hear. Be attuned to the "voices" attracting your attention. Identify and remove any distractions that affect your concentration. Take a pause. Wait for guidance from God.

Allow your mind to see God's vision for the situation. Ask God to connect you with others who can help you to achieve God's purposes and plans. God will give you discernment to know what portion of the decision you are to deal with and what part you should let go of and let the people involved in the situation work out.

Be mindful. A person with a strong independent spirit who has an "I will just do it myself" mentality will often go outside boundaries and not permit others to step in and help. If you are that person, ask God to teach you the right way to set boundaries and be secure enough within yourself to let others help. Learn to be collaborative. Integrate others to bring together the fullness of God's vision for the situation.

Showing compassion for others and being gracious, kind, and polite when interacting with others will keep us within God's boundaries.

KEEP YOUR MIND ON THE GOAL

Delays are a form of distraction. Delays caused by starting to do something else before completing the assignment are distractions. Be alert—stay focused. Keeping busy for the sake of doing something is not productive. An acronym for "busy" is "being under Satan's yoke." Strive to avoid actions that keep you busy and keep you from the timely completion of the mission at hand.

Sometimes a person may keep busy to hide the fact the person does not have the skills to accomplish the assignment. Rather than admit it or ask for help, the person begins to do something else, which may be beneficial, but it delays the assignment's completion. When you notice a team member is not working on the assigned task, remind the person of the goal. Offer to help the person achieve the goal. Ask God for discernment before jumping to a conclusion. Ask God for a heart of grace.

When we love God with all our heart, soul, and strength and sing songs, psalms, and words of praise to Him, we get His attention. He hears us from Heaven. When we pray, God listens to us. When we seek God and search for Him with all our heart, we will find Him. He is standing at the door, knocking and waiting for an invitation to come in.

Conclusion

THROUGHOUT THIS BOOK, I HAVE sought to inspire you to desire spiritual insight and revelatory wisdom from God. Smith Wigglesworth often said, "God is more eager to answer than we are to ask." God wants to talk to us!

Often, God speaks through the gift of prophecy. This book shares how the gift of prophecy plays a vital role in the world today. This book explores the gift of hearing from God through the prophetic and growing closer with the Holy Spirit through this gift. It is my prayer that it inspires you to learn to discern God's voice.

In the preceding chapters, I shared practical active listening tools to help you develop your spiritual ears to hear and recognize the voice of God. These tools are also great for you to master your listening skills in all environments.

I outlined proven methods to improve your active listening skills in Section 1. Guidelines on how prophetic people meditate on and study the Bible were discussed in Section 2. Discerning dreams, visions, and revelations prepared you in Section 3 to ask God for the interpretation. After all, God is more eager to answer than we are to ask! Section 4 covered how vital worship and prayer are to God. Finally, Section 5 provided you with an opportunity to complete a root cause analysis to obtain answers from God on matters of concern to you personally.

Throughout the book, you read examples of how, during our everyday lives, we hear and act in response to hearing the voice of God. You received guidance on how to develop strategies to take action on the revelation you receive from God.

I hope this book has inspired you to be as eager to hear the voice of God as He is to answer you. Let those

Conclusion

who have ears to hear—listen. God loves us, and He wants to communicate with us and through us!

I pray this book has equipped you with new listening skills to discern the voice of God to speak accurately in the spiritual authority God has released during this era of speaking. May God richly bless you always!

> *Do not merely listen to the word, and so deceive yourselves. Do what it says. Anyone who listens to the word but does not do what it says is like someone who looks at his face in a mirror and, after looking at himself, goes away and immediately forgets what he looks like. But whoever looks intently into the perfect law that gives freedom and continues in it-not forgetting what they have heard but doing it--they will be blessed in what they do (James 1:22–25).*

REFERENCES

INTRODUCTION
Karen Blanks Adams, *Life in the Matrix: Are you really in control of your decisions?* (Lake Mary, FL: Creation House, 2010)

SECTION ONE
Gwen Osborne, *God is My Banker Spiritual Strategy for Entrepreneurs,* Texarkana, AR: Phao Books, 2020)
KJV for King James Version

SECTION TWO
Ryrie Study Bible, New American Standard, (Chicago, IL: The Moody Bible Institute, 1978)
Life Application Study Bible, New International Version, (Wheaton, IL: Tyndale House Publishers, Inc., 2005)

SECTION THREE

Watchman Nee, *Spiritual Authority,* (New York, NY: Christian Fellowship Publishers, 1972)

Barbie Breathitt, *Revelatory Encounters,* (North Richland Hills, TX: Breath of the Spirit Ministries, Inc., 2006)

Chuck D. Pierce and Rebecca Wagner Sytsema, *When God Speaks*, (Ventura, CA: Regal Books, 2005)

Barbie L. Breathitt, *Dream Encounters, Seeing Your Destiny from God's Perspective*, (North Richland Hills, TX: Breath of the Spirit Ministries Enterprises, LLC., 2009)

Adam F. Thompson and Adrian Beale, *Divinity Code to Understanding Your Dreams and Visions*, (Shippensburg, PA: Destiny Image Publishers, Inc., 2011)

SECTION FOUR

John Dickson and Chuck D. Pierce, *Worship as It Is in Heaven,* (Ventura CA: Regal Books, 2010)

NASB for *New American Standard Bible*, (La Habra, CA: The Lockman Foundation, 1995).

References

NKJV for *New King James Version*, (Nashville, TN: Thomas Nelson Publishers, 1982)

Chuck D. Pierce, *Interpreting the Times: How God intersects with our lives to bring revelation and understanding*, (Lake Mary, FL: Charisma House, 2008)

SECTION FIVE

Ed Silvoso, *That None Should Perish*, (Ventura, CA: Regal Books, 1994)

KJV for King James Version

NIV for *The Holy Bible, New International Version*, (Grand Rapids, MI: Zondervan Publishing House, International Bible Society, 1984)

AMP for *The Amplified Bible*, (La Habra, CA: The Lockman Foundation, 1987)

MSG for *The Message, The Bible in Contemporary Language*, (Eugene H. Peterson, 2002)

TPT for *The Passion Translation*, (Savage, MN: BroadStreet Publishing Group, LLC. Trademark of Passion & Fire Ministries, Inc, 2020)

NKJV for *New King James Version*, (Nashville, TN: Thomas Nelson Publishers, 1982)